Coloring Your Way
to Better English

Coloring Your Way
to Better English

Larry W. Hilliard

iUniverse

COLORING YOUR WAY TO BETTER ENGLISH

iUniverse books may be ordered through booksellers or by contacting:

iUniverse
1663 Liberty Drive
Bloomington, IN 47403
www.iuniverse.com
844-349-9409

ISBN: 978-1-5320-8667-0 (sc)
ISBN: 978-1-5320-8666-3 (e)

Library of Congress Control Number: 2020904712

Print information available on the last page.

iUniverse rev. date: 11/12/2021

This book is dedicated to my mother, father and
my sister who were taken much to soon.

1. Use love and patience to teach.
2. Start any place in the coloring book.
3. Look for signs of improvement of any kind
4. Let the child know that you and the child are in it together.
5. Always let the child develop in his or her own time.
6. Celebrate good learning with good times.

Contents

Contents

NOUNS

Nouns

Nouns are the names of persons, places, things, or ideas.[1]

Persons

Places: tree house

Things: bike

Ideas: love, hope, caring, and friendship

Different Types of Nouns

There are proper, common, and collective nouns.

Proper Nouns: Mr. Smith's house[2]

Common Nouns: trees, people, cars, schools

Collective Nouns: team

Odd Things about Nouns

To make a noun plural, in most cases, just add an "s" to indicate more than one thing. For example, add an "s" to "home" makes "homes," meaning more than one.

Sometimes, however, you need to add an "es" to a noun to make it plural. For example, to make "bench" plural, you must add "es," making it "benches."

And for nouns ending in "y," you often change the "y" to "i" and then add "es." So "family" becomes "families."

Tip

Nouns with an "s" are always plural.

Nouns without an "s" are always singular.

Let's Review

Nouns are things that you can see, touch, hear, or taste.
And they are things you think about, such as love, hope, joy.
Nouns can be counted, and they can be a singular object.

VERBS

Verbs are words that express action, a state of being, or a condition.[2]

Action: playing

State of being: happy face

Condition: The truck has a flat.

Verbs have tense. There are six tenses in verbs: past, present, future, perfect past, perfect present, and perfect future.

Past tense: It was broken yesterday.

Present tense: reading

Future tense: going some place

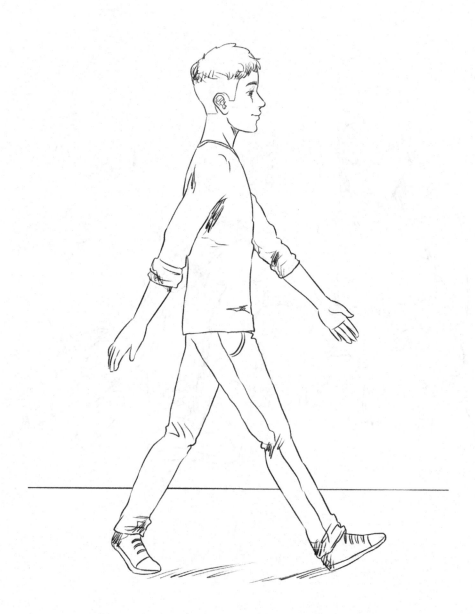

Perfect past tense: The action is in the past. It has the word *had* plus the past tense word. For example: I wish I had called yesterday, but I got busy.

Perfect present tense: The action is in the present. It has the extra words *have* or *has* plus the past tense. For example: It is a good day; it has been a fun day at the park.

Perfect future tense: The action is in the future; it has the extra words *will* or *shall* plus the past tense words. For example: Fred will run to third base as soon as his sneezing fit ends.[8]

Verbs have two voices: active and passive.[2]

Active: Larry throws the ball.

Passive: The ball was thrown by Larry.

Verbs also have moods: indicative, imperative, and subjunctive.

Indicative mood is used to make a statement or ask a question.[3]

I love ice cream.

Do you have any ice cream?

Do you like
ice cream?

Imperative mood is used to make a command, a request, or a suggestion.[3]

Please bring me my shoes.

Can I see you today?

You should put the milk in the glass before you drink it.

Subjunctive mood is used for hypothetical or conditional situations.[3]

If I had more money, I could buy my mother something for her birthday.

ADJECTIVES
AND ADVERBS

Adjectives

Adjectives modify nouns, pronouns, and other adjectives.[2]

Nouns

(These are directions for the child.)
You can describe the house any way you want to. You can color the house any way you want to.

It is a brown house.
It is a big house.

Person
Nouns

You can describe your friends.
My friends are tall.
short.
big.
small.

Adverbs

Adverbs modify verbs, adjectives, or other adverbs.[1] Adverbs answer the question of when, where, how, why, in what order, or how often.

When: We can play catch tomorrow. ← adverbs

I will be home *soon.* ← adverb

Where: Deliver all mail *here.*[1] ← adverb

How: She replied *quickly* and *angrily*.[1] ← adverbs

Why: Consequently, I left.[1] ← adverb

In what order:

      ↳ adverb

The *next* one in line will be the winner.

How often: ↦ adverb

He *seldom* did any work.

Let's Review

Remember—adjectives modify nouns, pronouns, and other adjectives. Adverbs modify adjectives or another adverb. Adverbs answer the questions of when, where, how, why, in what order, or how often.

COLORING
SENTENCE
PATTERNS

Coloring Sentence Patterns

Sentences are written in patterns. There are five patterns.

First Pattern
The first pattern is just subject and verb,[4] action auxiliary.

Subject

I	We
You	You
He, She, It	They
Who	

Verb

Past	
Present	
Future	

Joe slept

Subject	Verb
Joe	Slept

The Second Pattern[4]

Subject	+	Verb	+	Direct Object

I   eat   cake

The Third Pattern

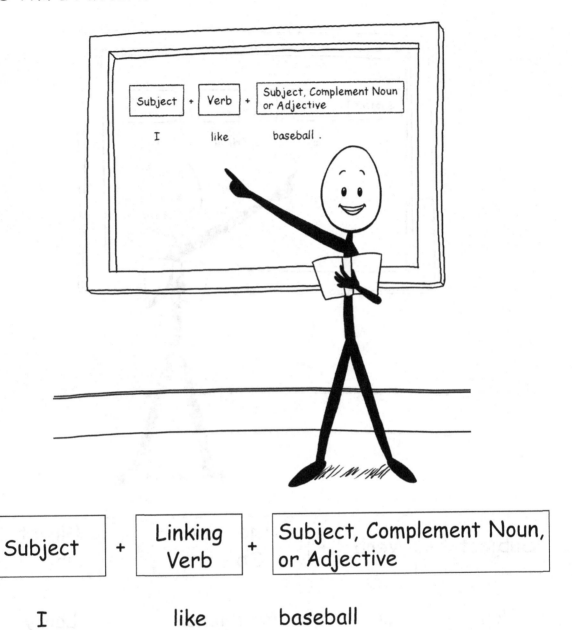

Subject	+	Linking Verb	+	Subject, Complement Noun, or Adjective

I   like   baseball

The Fourth Pattern

Subject	+	Verb	+	Indirect Object	+	Direct Object
You		are		my friend		Larry

The Fifth Pattern

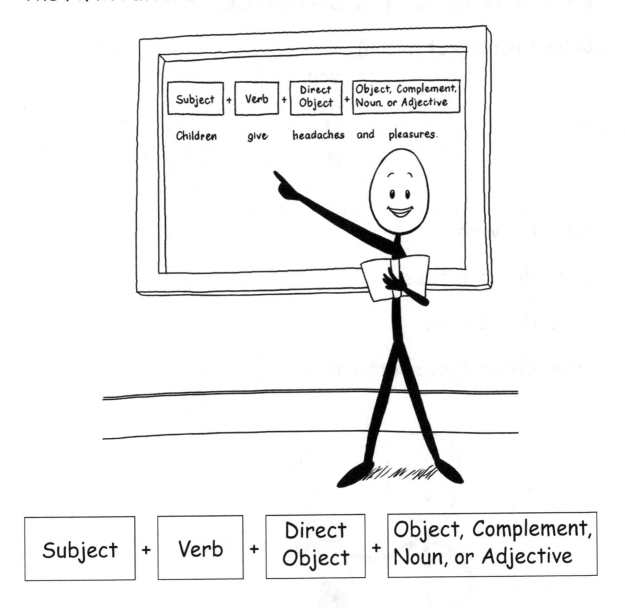

Subject	Verb	Direct Object	Object, Complement, Noun or Adjective

Children give headaches and pleasures

Let's Make a Sentence

Color the subject (Noun)   I
                                    you
                                    he
                                    she
                                    it

Color the verb

Color the adjectives

Color the adverbs

Color the sentence patterns

Putting It All Together

Think about the things you love.

I love playing.

_ _ _ _

_ _ _ _

_ _ _ _

_ _ _ _

Think about the things you have

I have a truck.

_ _ _ _

_ _ _ _

Putting It All Together, Continues

SPELLING— CONSONANTS AND VOWELS

Spelling—Consonants and Vowels

There are consonants.

Consonants are anything that are not vowels.[5]

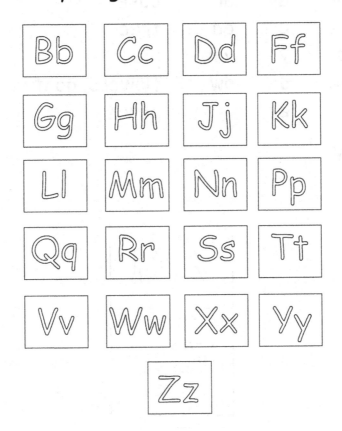

Bb	Pp
Cc	Qq
Dd	Rr
Ff	Ss
Gg	Tt
Hh	Vv
Jj	Ww
Kk	Xx
Ll	Yy
Mm	Zz
Nn	

Vowels

Vowels are anything other than consonants.[3]

Aa	→ a-e	ay	ai	cake
Ee	→ e-e	e	ea	tree
Ii	→ i-e	y	iah	pie
Oo	→ o-e	oa	ow	flowers, goat
Uu	→ ue	ew		new

Sometimes Y

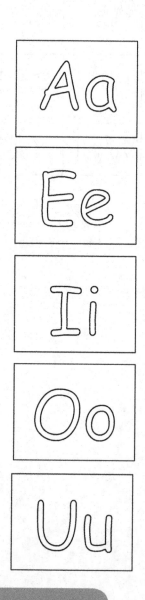

Think Before You Spell

If you want to spell "house," you have to think about a house.

And now the sounds of consonants and vowels. So, an h sound. Then you need a vowel, then a consonant, and then a vowel.

This would be a great time to use the dictionary.

Think before you spell!

Remember—

1. Think about what you want to spell. In our example, "house".
2. Pronounce the first letter, which is a consonant. Then you need a vowel between each consonant.

Say the word slowly.

Punctuation

Punctuation tells the reader to stop, rest, and ask questions.[7]

Stop

Use at the end of a statement.
    I like cake. ← Full stop

Rest

Use at the end of a statement and the beginning of the next one.
    I like cake, and I like to play ball.
       ↳ a comma

Punctuation

?

The question mark is used to ask questions.

;

The semicolon is used to connect to statements that do not have and,

> but,
> or,
> nor,
> so,
> yet,
> while,
> whereas,

:

The colon is used to start a list.

Common Mistakes

1. Not sure about what a noun is.[6]
2. Not sure about what verbs are.
3. Not putting an ending on verbs.
4. Not sure what a subject and verb are.
5. Don't know the different between adjective and adverbs.
6. Not sure about punctuation.

1. Use love and patience to teach.
2. Start any place in the coloring book.
3. Look for signs of improvement of any kind
4. Let the child know that you and the child are in it together.
5. Always let the child develop in his or her own time.
6. Celebrate good learning with good times.

Bibliography

1. Leggett, Glenn, Mead, David, and Kramer, Melinda G. Prentice Hall *Handbook for Writers*: 11th ed. Englewood Cliffs, New Jersey, 1991.

2. Baugh, L. Sue, *Essentials of English Grammar:* The quick guide to good English, 3rd ed. New York, 2005.

3. Haslem, John A. *Webster's New World Notebook Grammar and Punctuation Guide.* 1st ed. 1998.

4. Fowler, Ramsey H., Aaron, Jane E. *The Little, Brown Handbook.* 12th ed. New Jersey: Pearson 2012.

5. Schoolfield, Lucille D., Timberlake, Josephine B. *Better Speech and Better Reading:* Boston, Massachusetts: Expression Company. 1972.

6. Berry, Thomas E. *The Most Common Mistakes in English Usage.* Boston, Massachusetts: McGraw-Hill: 1971.

7. Alward, Edgar C., Alward, Jean A. *Punctuation Plan & Simple:* New York: Barnes & Noble.1997.

8. Woods, Geraldine. *English Grammar for Dummies.* 2nd ed. John Wiley & sons, Inc. Hoboken, New, Jersey. 2010.

9. Corbett, Edward P.J. *The Little English Handbook,* 3rd ed. John Wiley & sons Inc. New York. 1980.

Printed in the United States
by Baker & Taylor Publisher Services